HE SEES ME

THE BROKEN ROAD THAT LED ME TO MY KING

LAURA HAUSMAN

Halo
PUBLISHING
INTERNATIONAL

ISBN: 978-1-61244-630-1
Library of Congress Control Number: 2018905969

Printed in the United States of America

Halo Publishing International
1100 NW Loop 410
Suite 700 - 176
San Antonio, Texas 78213
1-877-705-9647
www.halopublishing.com
contact@halopublishing.com

DEDICATION

First and foremost, I give my sincere gratitude to my Lord and Savior, Jesus Christ. Thank You for coming to see about me that day and for pouring Your love so tenderly into my heart. In Your presence, I find rest; in Your presence, my soul is at peace.

To my three incredibly beautiful, talented, loving, kind, gentle children—Tayler, Derek and Ava Grace—words can't express the love and joy you have each brought to my life.

Tayler, thank you for reminding me of all the good that is in me. You have been my greatest cheerleader. Even in our roughest times, I knew you were in the background praying and believing in me. You were my first baby, and you stole my heart from the moment I laid eyes on you. I can't wait to see what the Lord has planned for you. When you become weary, and life becomes hard, and your heart begins to break, I promise that if you just lean on Him, surrender to Him, He will lead you through the valley. You are an amazing young lady, and you will find your way in all things. Do not settle for one ounce less than what God says you deserve, and that is a whole lot! You are the apple of His eye; wait on the Lord. Again, I say: Wait on the Lord. "Those who wait on the Lord shall renew their strength; they shall mount up with wings like eagles, they shall run and not be weary; they shall walk and not faint" (Isaiah 40:31). I love you to the moon and the stars!

Derek, thank you for always being the laugh I need in the good and the bad times. You've softened the blows of many of my heartaches with your smile and your sense of humor. Thank you for your undeniable respect for me and for becoming such an amazing young man. I have every faith in you, in your talents, and in your abilities. You have something great to give to others; you have something to offer that nobody else does. Spend time seeking your talents and gifts, and then once you find them, use them, and go after them with all your heart and soul. You were not called to anything short of greatness. I know you will find this greatness inside of yourself, and I promise you it will be more than you can ever imagine. As Proverbs 18:6 states, "A Man's gift makes room for Him, and brings Him before great men." He created you for AMAZING THINGS! And, the answer is, "YES, I AM STILL ON THAT GOD KICK." Remember Jeremiah 1:4: "I knew you BEFORE I formed you in your mother's womb." And Jeremiah 29:11 says, "'I know the plans I have for you,' says the LORD, 'plans to prosper you and not to harm you, plans to give you hope and a future.'" I love you to the moon and the stars!

Ava Grace: What can I say about my Ava Grace? You are my little miracle ball that is here by the grace of God; you are something special. I thank God that I was able to introduce you to Him and the Holy Spirit at such a young age. You embody the spirit of the Lord. You carry His love so beautifully, so openly, and I know this is how God wants us all to be. Matthew 18:3-4 says, "I tell you the truth, unless you turn from your sins and become like little children, you will never enter the Kingdom of Heaven. So, anyone who becomes as humble as this little child is the greatest in the Kingdom of Heaven." You shine this truth so brightly and remind me of what this verse looks like. You have a special blessing on your life, and I know that you will do great things for the Kingdom and for God. When you are no longer a child, and you find yourself at any point in your life, at a crossroads, always, always remember Jesus and that He has your heart and life in His hands. He is your home, and He will never leave you or fail you. I love you to the moon and the stars and to Jesus Christ's heart, blood, and love.

There are so many people who have made a huge impact on my journey, and I can't begin to list them all. But, I need to mention a few: To my first and best friend in the world, Mary Kendall. You have walked with me through every storm, through every joy, and you have seen me at my best and loved me despite my worst times. I can't thank you enough for your continued love, support, and encouragement.

There are many people that have prayed for me and with me regarding situations in my life and for the people that are so very close to my heart. I can't begin to list them all. There are no words to adequately express my gratitude for all the countless prayers, for being an ear to hear and an open heart to love me, no matter what I was facing or going through. #LIFERS

There are too many pastors to list that have guided me, loved me, inspired me, and spoken life into me over the years. First and foremost, I want to thank Bishop Joey Johnson, who has been instrumental in my walk with Christ. Bishop, you have provided so much wisdom and imparted so much guidance into my life. I would not be who I am today if not for your teaching, your love, and your prayers. Much love to you!

Pastor Mayceo Smith and First Lady Patrice Smith: where do I begin?! The two of you have blessed me richly. I was led to City of Joy during a very difficult time in my life, and from the first time I walked through the doors, I have felt nothing but love and acceptance. Your generosity towards Ava and me came at a very crucial time in our lives, and we are forever grateful to you both for loving us and truly caring about us. Keep doing what you do; the Lord is well pleased. I love you both!

CONTENTS

FOREWORD

Often it takes time to fully understand and begin to see how God will take our life experiences and turn them around for goodness and purpose. Because dark and disappointing seasons can so deeply affect us, we must rely on the assurance and hope that God will indeed use our dark days for ultimate blessing in this life. We may not have access to every detail, but we can fully trust that through the moments of contrast, our uniquely beautiful testimony is crafted. While we are being molded, our faith is strengthened, our roots are deepened, and greatness sustains us when strong winds blow.

By revisiting private, tender events from her distant and recent past, Laura Hausman grips us and gently walks us through her road to healing, forgiveness, wholeness, and self-exploration with honesty and candor. Whether as a daughter, wife, mother, or as a woman fighting for her emotional and spiritual freedom, she inspires us to think about and connect with our intimate stories that set the stage for personal endurance, triumph, and legacy.

Each chapter works in tandem to teach us how a fragile little girl blossoms into a woman, even more determined to become who God predestined her to be. We travel with her through chapters of her recorded experiences to be reminded that God is always with us, longing to speak to us and navigate us through hurtful, blissful, exciting and frightening times.

Upon completion of this book, you will be challenged to revisit your life's story and search for God's handprint actively at work. Prepare to be amazed by how very present God has been and continues to be as we journey through this gift of life.

Tameaka Reid Simms
Pastor, Author

INTRODUCTION

He came to see about me, to inquire about me.

He came to see after me, to attend to and take care of me.

He came to see me through, to stay with me to the end,
'til completion, 'til eternity.

To know Him is to love Him; to love Him is to trust Him.

To trust Him IS EVERYTHING.

Hello, beautiful ones. I am humbled that you have decided to purchase this book and are allowing me to share my story with you. I do not take it lightly that you have taken your resources and time to bless me and this labor of love. My prayer is that something about my story resonates with you, touches your heart, and more importantly leads you to the cross where you will find all you've ever searched for, all you've ever needed. There is nothing special about my story; we all have a story to tell. God has merely given me the courage, strength, and talent to put mine on paper, to be a blessing to others. God will always see you through every vision He gives you. I spent so many years fearing life, thinking I could not accomplish all these things that were bubbling up in my heart to do. And, by myself, I can't do them; it's only with God's strength and His wisdom that I can endure, thrive, and succeed infinitely more than, far greater than I could ever imagine. He gave me hope when I could not see an end to my pain. He gave me love when all I could feel was emptiness. He gave me grace when all I could see were my mistakes. He gave me faith when I was filled with fear. I invite you, with my humble and grateful heart, to join me on this journey to free your soul and become who God created you to be. For you were once lost, but now you are found, secure in the arms of the One who will never leave you and never forsake you.

WHERE IT ALL BEGAN

"Before I formed you in the womb I knew you,

before you were born I set you apart;

I appointed you as a prophet to the nations." (Jeremiah 1:5)

I am not sure where one begins when writing a book about their life, with all its heartaches, disappointments, unanswered prayers, and of course all its happiness, joy and fulfillment. But I am going to take a stab at doing just that. My first thought is whether anyone cares to read about my life. I mean, who am I really? I am just another soul on this planet who has managed to make it to mid-life with my heart somewhat intact and my body still running pretty well. I will admit there have been times when I didn't think my heart or my body was going to have the strength to see another day. There were times when I could physically feel my heart breaking. You know those gut-wrenching times in life when even breathing becomes difficult. I have come to understand fully just how connected our minds and bodies are. It is true that what we feel in our hearts will manifest itself in our physical being, as well, eventually. I have also come to know just how fleeting life is. One day I was a ten-year-old little girl, and then seemingly in the blink of an eye, I was the mother of a ten-year-old. Looking back, I can now pinpoint that it was at the age of ten that I first felt the spirit of the Lord. The thing is, I had no idea what I was feeling. It was a beautiful fall day, and I was on a field trip to Mary Campbell's Cave, in Cuyahoga Falls, Ohio. I was sitting at a picnic table eating the lunch my mom had packed for me when I felt something in my insides. I say insides because, at the time, I had no idea that I had a "spirit", I just knew that something had swept over me. I can only explain it as to say that "something" or "someone" came to tell me that I was special, that I was loved, that I was going to make a difference in people's lives, that I was simply and utterly adored, that my life was going to be amazing. Of course, I now know this was the Holy Spirit tapping me on my shoulder and letting me know that I had been chosen, that God was seeing me, and that He indeed loved me. I didn't give this moment much thought at the time, other than recognizing how amazing I felt in that moment. I finished my lunch and went back to being a normal ten-year-old girl enjoying my field trip. I do remember feeling more excitement that day than I ever had before.

THE ROOTS

"God says through Moses: 'These commandments I give you this day are to be upon your hearts, and you shall teach them diligently to your children at all times." (Deuteronomy 6)

"Bring your children up in the training and admonition of the Lord." (Ephesians 6:4)

My parents were both 18 when they got married. My mom was pregnant with my sister, and I am certain this was the reason for the marriage. I don't know if love was ever a part of their union; I'm not sure if it can even be called a union. I have memories of my mother seemingly head over heels for my father and desperately wanting his love in return. I am not sure why, but he never reciprocated this love back to her, no matter what she tried to say or do. And she tried hard for nearly 18 years. I remember wondering why he didn't love her, why he didn't hug or kiss her, and why they were always fighting. Why is mom always crying? Why are my sister and I sleeping with my mom? Why is my Dad not home again tonight? Where is my Dad? Why does my mom keep trying? Why does she allow him to treat her so poorly? Why? I had so many questions that I had no answers for. I now know how deeply this dysfunctional marriage affected me, and how much it played a role in my own personal, intimate relationships. This was my example of love and relationships.

I don't have too many pleasant memories of my childhood. Please don't get me wrong: I was well taken care of; I was fed, clothed, and I do know my parents loved me. But the kind of love that a child needs, the tenderness, the affirmations of worth, the glowing adoration and ability to give it, the necessary time and all the other things that children require were indeed in lack. I would never say I was abused, nor do I feel I was, but I missed out on love shaping me as a young girl. In fact, I have huge periods of my childhood that I cannot recall.

After I had my own children, I began to think about my childhood. I wanted to know what kind of little girl I was, what my strengths, weaknesses, likes, and dislikes were. Did I make funny faces? What were my embarrassing stories? What were my favorite things I did with my parents? What were our family traditions? What were our core beliefs as a family? I wanted to know so much more. I tried to remember myself and my life back then. What was Laura the little girl like? I wanted to know her. I desperately searched for memories, for any of those things I just mentioned above...anything at all. I was looking for any tiny memorable, joyful moment.

One day, as I was trying to remember, I realized I couldn't recall any of these times, events, or things because they never occurred; they simply didn't exist in my world. I remember being filled with so much sadness at this truth that I cried until my eyes were mere slits, swollen like I had been stung by the fiercest bee on the planet. And then, I went to the other painful place and asked myself why. Why did I not have these memories that seemingly every normal, red-blooded child had and could rewind in their minds and enjoy again and again? Of course, I know I was exaggerating because every child doesn't have these memories. But it felt and looked that way to me. I wanted to know why. Why did I not have these? I had no memories of story time; no memories of tea parties; no memories of days at the park or trips to the zoo; no special family traditions or family outings; no memories of goodnight kisses from my father or memories of sessions of laughter until my cheeks couldn't take it anymore; no days of marathon movie watching or memories of bonding and connecting as a family. I only had horrible, painful memories. Memories of my

Mom and Dad breaking up, seemingly every other month; Dad moving out; Dad moving back in; Dad cheating on Mom; Mom begging him to come back home; Mom then cheating on Dad; Mom driving around looking for Dad while my sister and I were in our jammies in the backseat; Mom taking us into bars searching for Dad; Mom taking us to wait outside a hotel for my Dad to come out; Dad begging me at the back door to let him in because my Mom locked him out; countless fights and arguments; Mom working two and three jobs to make ends meet; Dad jumping from one job to another; Dad getting a babysitter so he could go out while he was supposed to be taking care of us. Yeah, I had a bag full of *those* memories, and that sad fact has plagued my life and relationships for as long as I can remember. I am angry and hurt. This anger and hurt followed me into every intimate relationship I ever had.

After nearly 18 years of marriage, my parents finally divorced. I am fully aware that my childhood could have been way worse. I could have been physically abused, sexually abused, and so much more; but it is important for me to convey here the serious damage that is done to a child's spirit when they do not experience the love and nurturing that is expected and desperately needed. And this lack affects every area of their lives, well into adulthood. It's like a never-ending search for your identity, for your worth, for approval, for adoration. It's an exhausting and heartbreaking search. I have spent the better part of my adult life emotionally damaged and searching for something or someone to heal my broken heart and fill me up.

In the Middle: Searching

"You will seek me and find me when you seek me
with all your heart." (Jeremiah 29:13)

I then went about life. Life just seemed to roll on from that day.
The following chapters will take you on my journey, but years would
pass before I would surrender my life, my heart, my everything to
the Spirit, to my Heavenly Father, who had come to see about
me that day on the picnic bench when I was just a ten-year-old
little girl. I had grown up without an earthly father's attention,
adoration, or affection, though I desperately sought this and more
from him. I believe that all little girls need attention from their
fathers. I believe it is at the core of who we become as women.
There is a certain level of confidence gained by having a father
who nurtures our hearts, our emotions; when our father simply
adores us and makes sure we are aware of his affections for us,
we learn by example how we are to be treated by a man, what to
expect from a man, what we can count on from a man, and how
vulnerable we can be with a man. A father is the first man to show
us our worth as little girls, which directly carries us into knowing
what our worth is as women. Therefore, when we do not have the
proper example from the beginning, we go on an endless search
to fill the gaping hole in our hearts. I now know that no human
being can ever fulfill the desires of our hearts; no human being can
ever show us our worth. Yes, earthly fathers have a responsibility
to pour as much love, adoration, and affection that they can into
their daughter's hearts, but there is only ONE who can fully,
radically, and completely love, adore, and cherish you: Jesus Christ,
my Lord, my Savior, my everything.

It was around the age of 18 that I recognized the Empty Giant
inside my soul. I was damaged, broken, and I had no idea what to

do about it. So, I did what I was used to doing, seeking to be filled up by relationships, by sexual encounters, by men, by drinking and partying. I desperately wanted the love of a man; I had a huge gaping hole in my heart that my father neglected to fill, and I was deceived into believing this would work. As young girls, we crave the love and attention from our earthly fathers. It is essential to our well-being and our hearts. When this is missing, we set out on a never-ending journey to find this lost father love, searching in places that lead only to more heartache. And in the end, we give up our innocence, our hearts, and parts of our souls to consistently empty, unfulfilling sexual encounters, drugs, alcohol, and many other destructive patterns. My search always landed me in sexual encounters. One day I woke up and counted the losses I had suffered through my promiscuity, the parts of my heart that were gone, the parts of my soul that I freely gave away with nothing to gain in return. I had essentially suffered a loss with each and every one. I began to ask myself why in the world I kept participating in something that I had absolutely nothing to gain from. No joy, no peace, no sense of fulfillment, no edification, nothing. I walked away each time with less of my heart and soul. But God always provides.

My mother moved on to another relationship that took her to Florida, and I stayed behind living with my father at the age of 14. My mom later married that man, and I now know that God sent him not only to love my mom, but to love me, my sister, and my children.

Father's Day is a tough day for me. Over the years, as I have gone to buy a card for my father, none of them seemed to fit. They say things like, "Thank you for loving me well," "Thank you for guiding me," "Thank you for making me feel special," "Thank you for being my rock," "Thank you for showing me my beauty and worth," etc. None of that fit the description of my Dad. My heart so wanted one of those cards to be my reality, but all they did was make me cry and remind me of what I did not have in him. On Father's Day last year, this was my Facebook post:

Father's Day is not a day that brings me much Joy or Happiness. If I may be transparent and real...My Father has not been the best and did not nurture me and adore me the way in which all little girls need to feel from their Fathers, to let them know just how loved they are and how much they are worth. I continue to Love him in spite of the pain he caused....I guess we all do the Best we know how to do I wish him love, peace and all the happiness the world has to offer and I will Honor him as my Father. However, there is a man that I know the Lord brought to my Mother's Life, not only to Bless her but to bring to me and my sister more Love than we could contain......This is my Step Dad as society calls him, I call him, Papa. This man came into our lives when I was 14 years old and he has loved me beyond my wildest dreams, he extends his love and joy to me and my sister in more ways than we can count. He has been My Rock, My Shoulders to cry on, My Provider when needed, My Encouraging voice, My biggest fan, My set of strong hands whenever I need handy work done, My soft place to land... and he has taken on that role and provided all this to my 3 beautiful children and became their Papa too. We are not his blood daughters, or his blood grand-children...but you would never know it. This man has been the Grace, the Mercy, the Love that my mother and me and my sister so desperately needed and I Thank God for him. I would not be where I am today without My Papa. God saw fit to bring him to us and let me tell you, he can't even talk about any of us without tearing up, his love has no boundaries, if you ask him......we are HIS CHILDREN, PERIOD. I salute this man today, I commend him for his continual, unwavering Love, his stellar Character and his dedication to my mother and to me and my Children. This picture reveals his spirit, his love for life and for all of us. Papa, words can't express my gratitude to you...Thank you for lifting us up and showing us just what the Love of a Father really looks like. You are very special to each and every one of us. With Love...Your Daughter, Laura <3

Laura Hausman
Jul 5, 2011 at 11:21pm · ⊗

Papa....one of my favorite pictures!

📷   Write a comment...   ☺

22

ON THE WAY:
MARRIAGE (SAVE ME)

"Do not put your trust in princes, in human beings,
who cannot save." (Psalm 146:3)

So, at the age of 21, I got married. We had only known each other and been dating for three months when he proposed. And, I said yes. I don't believe I knew what I was saying yes to at the time. Remember the example I had of marriage. He was and is a great person: kind, loving, responsible, and so much more. He was a breath of fresh air especially after the disappointments I had endured in childhood and other failed relationships. I was just tickled at the thought of being a bride. But I know now I was more excited to have someone who was going to truly love me and take care of me. At this point, I was still empty, void of my earthly father's love, and desperately looking to fill that hole. And, I am still not saved, nor walking with the Lord. So, we married, and it was a beautiful wedding and honeymoon. Shortly after our wedding, we decided to move to Florida where my Mom and Papa were living at the time. It was a good relationship. We didn't fight, we had some common interests, and he adored me and loved me. Someone to adore me and love me: that's what I had been looking for, right? A man to adore me, cherish me, take care of me, and actually desire to do so. And he did all of this for me. By all accounts, I was filled up; at least I convinced myself I was.

But I merely pushed down that old, familiar Empty Giant and went about my life with him. It wasn't hard to do; as I said, he is a good man. It wasn't hard, but it wasn't right. At the time, I had no idea of the reality of the situation. It was just too painful to visit this empty place. And if his love could at least make me believe my emptiness was filled up, then so be it. Two years into our marriage, I became pregnant with our daughter. I was delighted at the thought of being a mom. There were so many things that I knew I wanted to do differently and so many things that I promised to be and do for my children. I welcomed that opportunity. She was born on July 9th, and she was the most beautiful thing I had ever laid my eyes on. She melted my heart and opened parts of my heart I never knew existed. She was also a great diversion for me to avoid searching myself and healing what needed to be healed. She was the cutest diversion I have ever allowed to keep me from doing work on myself! She brought so much joy, laughter, and love to my life, and she still does. She was and still is our baby girl! She was our shining light, our everything. We dedicated our time and love to her, and we were great parents and remain that for her even today.

It was about four years into our marriage that the ugly head of emptiness began to surface again. It never left; it was just buried and replaced by the demands of motherhood, work, and life in general. I confided in my best friend. She was my constant since the age of 13. She knows me, my family, my heart, and my heart aches. I began to express to her how I had been feeling. She knew all about my emptiness from my childhood, and she watched me on my search to fill this void. But I know she was hoping this marriage was what I was missing, as I had hoped, too. I was feeling lost, lonely, empty, and I had a sense that something was missing. I began to spend time talking things out with her and trying to get mind clear on what was happening and why I was feeling this way again. There were moments that I felt better, but I never felt quite right. I pushed all the "not quite right" feelings down and just kept things moving.

I began to notice the disconnection that I felt in the marriage and had been feeling for a while. But I never wanted my kids to experience a broken family, and divorce wasn't something I wanted to entertain. I ignored it and pushed it down as far as I could for as long as I could. Then in 1995, I got pregnant. I was very upset and concerned because I was having uneasy, complicated, and hard to explain feelings about the marriage. On March 12th, I gave birth to my son, Derek Lee. Joy, joy, joy is all I could feel when I looked at his little face. We were again elated to be parents. After all, we were great parents, and we did that very well together. Boys were rare in my family, so having a boy was an awesome, wonderful surprise. He was just as amazing to us as his sister. When I tell you that these two precious souls lit up my world that is an understatement! They became my world and were beautiful inside and out.

After settling into being a mom to a little one again, the ugly monster of emptiness showed himself to be bigger and uglier than before. I began to go out with friends for drinks, dinner, or whatever. I thought that maybe I just needed to get out and be myself for a little while instead of being a mom and wife all the time. I thought that would make everything okay and that was all I needed. Again, I was pushing down the emptiness; I did not want to face it. It was just too painful and too much to digest.

ROADBLOCK: DIVORCE

"Your beauty and love chase after me every day of my life."
(Psalm 23:6)

After months of going out and having fun with my friends, I decided, at the suggestion of my husband, to enroll in college. I had always loved school and always wanted to go to college. But, as a young girl, I was never pushed or motivated towards my education. Although I was an excellent, straight-A student, going to college wasn't a priority in my family. I enrolled in college and instantly fell in love with every aspect of it. I loved the campus, the education, the unique vibe that college has, all of it. I do have many nerd qualities, and perhaps that is why. I started classes in the fall and thought that this was the missing piece. I needed to begin to stimulate my brain and achieve some of my lifelong goals. But that ugly thing would not leave me. That nasty, dark, cold mess I call the Empty Giant was always reminding me it had gone nowhere.

By this time, my marriage was really in trouble. We were not connecting in any way other than our children. I became very distant and aloof emotionally, physically, and in every way. My husband was supportive for so long, but he hit his breaking point and began really to be affected by the ugliness of my Empty Giant. He knew I was no longer there, and he was gracious and mature enough to do what I couldn't do. He wrote me a letter and explained his heart and what he knew to be true about what was happening with me, with us. At that, we separated and filed for divorce. It was the beginning of a long road called "guilt" for me. The bags of guilt that I carried for this lasted well into my

26

next relationship, and to be honest, some guilt never goes away. Our divorce was as smooth as any divorce could go. We had the same attorney; we fought over nothing because the only thing that mattered to us both in the midst of the pain and hurt was the hearts of our children. We placed them and their well-being at the forefront of our lives. We still partnered together to raise them as a team. There is always hurt and consequences to a divorce; and children are affected by divorce, no matter how maturely it is handled.

Our children lived very normal lives when it came to divorce. Even the teachers at their conferences were shocked to find out that we weren't married because they could not see any signs that pointed to them coming from a broken home. And for that, I am more than grateful. He loved me well, he was and is an amazing man, he is one of my greatest friends, and we have a great friendship today. We have raised two incredibly beautiful children, and he will always be loved by me and be a very important person in my life. I wouldn't be who I am today without the help he gave me and the love he showed me.

It was near the end of my divorce that I met my second husband in college. Still not saved, I fell right into the same trap, the same pit, and chose a relationship, a man for all the wrong reasons. I dated him and lived with him for nearly ten years. I know now that my reasons and desires were horribly superficial and still had everything to do with my Empty Giant. After about ten years, we broke up.

ON THE WAY II: SAVED

Jesus answered, "I am the way and the truth and the life. No one comes to the Father except through me." (John 14:6)

"Salvation is found in no one else, for there is no other name under heaven given to mankind by which we must be saved." (Acts 4:12)

So, here I am, alone and starting all over again. And, again, the Empty Giant is all around me and, I am beginning to wonder if it will ever be gone. I am devastated by the ending of this long relationship and trying to work through the pain and heartache of it all. I believe something happens to our hearts when our lives are hit with such traumatic change. Not only was there the loss of the relationship, but there was also an uprooting of our home; we had to leave the house that had become somewhat familiar to us and begin again somewhere new. And, "new" doesn't always equate to an easy or good feeling. When we hear the word "new", it seems to have a positive connotation to it, but it is not always a positive thing. Change is the one thing we can all count on in life, and it seemed to follow me everywhere I went (at least every 7-10 years.) So, I dusted myself off, as I had become accustomed to doing and had gotten pretty good at too, and I marched on. I was still the same dedicated, loving mother that I had always been; that was a constant and was not changing. I also had a career change and was still desperately trying to get my degree. I had taken several years off due to my first divorce, and now this situation had set me back with college as well. But every chance I got, I would enroll part-time and plug away at this college thing. I changed my major three times so you know the road became longer than it should have been. I began to meditate often and read the teachings of Buddha, which I found to be very enlightening and peaceful. I believe that there is much to gain in meditation and the silence of the mind. Still, I was unfulfilled. I wasn't banking on those Buddhist teachings to fill me up and eradicate my Empty Giant, but there were times that they helped immensely.

Anytime that a relationship ends you begin to search yourself and ask what your role was in the demise; if you aren't careful you begin sliding down that slippery slope toward thinking the "it was all my fault" lie. I kind of slid down that slide, so I wanted the relationship back. I set out to repair, restore, and get a second chance with him. It was during those three years apart from him that the Lord found me. Yes, He found me; I don't believe we go seeking the Lord. I believe He finds us, and we either choose to respond to Him, or we choose to ignore Him. It was a normal evening, and I was at home in my room. I was flipping the channel when the phone rang, so I stopped to answer it. When I came back into the room, it had landed on a channel where a very raspy-voiced lady was talking. She began to say that God loves you and He is waiting for you to come to know who He is, to surrender your life to Him, and to trust that He knows what is best for you. Will you accept His proposal today? Will you receive Him as your Lord and Savior? I stayed on the channel and listened to the rest of her message; I felt a lightness, a breakthrough come to my spirit. I was captivated by His love, and from that moment on, I gave my life to Christ. My spirit connected to His, and I knew at that moment that He was real and that I had found the missing piece, the eradicator of my Empty Giant. I wept and wept for hours that night. I gave my life to Him, and He began this amazing transformation in my heart, mind, and soul. I was, as they say, on fire for the Lord! My journey began, and I wrote this poem:

Spread your wings, open your eyes;
It's only a matter of time before you fly,
Say good-bye.

Spread your wings, enlarge your heart;
It's a chance to wake up,
A time to do your part.

Spread your wings, silence all the doubt;
It's a new path to take;
It's a new route.

Spread your wings, breathe it all in;
It's a new day—
You already WIN.

And, this one:

Somewhere beyond the pain
You'll know where you need to go.

Life will no longer be a strain;
Darkness must give in to the glow.
Breathe in deep
(His love is the only way;
All else is cheap).

The ultimate price He did pay;
Sit in His Presence; things become brighter.
You'll feel just like an angel
And oh, so much lighter.

For you are a child of God
And so deserve the BEST.

Search all over,
But you'll never find your rest!

I began this beautiful walk with the Lord. I bought a Bible, and I saturated myself in His word. I wanted to know all about this Man who told me He loved and adored me more than I could ever imagine. I am not sure if I was instantaneously filled up, but I can tell you that I was being filled up. Each day I was given more of His goodness, more of His strength. I was being built up by His amazing grace and mercy. He revealed things to me that I had never known about life and myself before. I was coming out of my dark place and finally beginning to see the big picture. He told me of things that were going to happen in the future. I call them little nuggets of goodness. They come to me like slideshow movies in my mind. He doesn't give it all away, for He knows I can't handle all of it at once, and He surely likes His children to be surprised from time to time. He told me there will be pleasure from all the pain that I have endured, and that even though He didn't cause all the heartache moments that happened to me, He was able to make something good out of every little thing that had ever broken my heart. And, my heart was broken. This realization hit me like a ton of bricks. I had been walking around for the better part of my adult life as a heartbroken little girl, still longing for the love that all little girls yearn to receive from their fathers. But, even though God found me and I accepted His invitation, I was still in process, still needing to be refined and purified. And, because of my inability to trust my earthly father, trusting God became a challenge for me in my walk with Him. God knew all that before He called me. He knew all my pain, all my heartache; He knew every tear I had ever cried, and He knew every tiny thing that my heart desired. He knew it all and still does. I kept pressing into His word, and I began to go to church. I found one that I went to for just a short while that did not seem to resonate with my spirit, so I kept searching. Then He answered my prayer to be reunited with the man I had just spent ten years of my life with. Don't get it twisted; God sometimes answers our prayers just to show us how wrong we were and how far away from His will for our lives we are.

SECOND MARRIAGE

"In his heart a man plans his course, but the LORD
determines his steps." (Proverbs 16:19)

After three years of being apart from him, I began to have the
drive and passion for reaching out to him, reconciling with him,
starting anew, and allowing us to experience what we had lacked
before. Remember, I am now saved, and I know the Lord, but I am
still not whole, nor healed up from my Empty Giant. The Empty
Giant goes right with me into this second marriage. I know I have
a healer, and I know that God is love and that He has a great plan
for my life. But I am still not fully trusting and accepting this in the
depths of my heart and soul. I am still relying on a *person* to fill
the empty place in my heart.

As believers, we daily need to be renewed, to spend time with the
Lord, to get to know Him, and this is exactly what my soul began
to desire. I walked into a church in my hometown of Akron, on a
rainy, cold day shortly after we began to talk again, and I knew I
had found my home. My spirit was immediately connected there,
and I began to be taught by one of the most intelligent, amazing
theologians in the country. I learned more about God and His word
from Bishop Joey Johnson than I can even really put into words. I
have been blessed to be a part of his teachings, to be able to make
some great friendships, and to connect with some amazing people.
I have been blessed to be a part of this ministry. It has carried
me through some very difficult times; the messages from Bishop
Johnson have strengthened me during many hardships. I will be
forever humbled and grateful for his guidance and leadership in

my life. I continued to press into the Lord; I was saved, but I was still broken.

We reentered our relationship, and by all accounts, I believed the Lord had answered my prayer to bring us back. I later realized that not all open doors come from the Lord, and if He does open them, sometimes it is only to reveal truths that our spirits need to know. I was delighted for the second chance, and I am convinced that it was the best thing that could have happened. I now know and understand that God sometimes allows things to take place in our lives to reveal that we are walking in our flesh and not following our spirits or His guidance. I also now know that God would never desire or bless a believer getting married to a non-believer. This is not His design. His word is clear about the unequally yoked union. I understand that a marriage where one spouse gets saved during the marriage and that this saved person can win over their spouse without a word. I get all that. And I understand that the Lord hates divorce and will guide that person to remain in the marriage. However, I am talking about entering into a marriage where one partner is saved already, and the other is not. To enter that marriage consciously aware that the Lord says not to is a clear sign that I am walking in my own desire and flesh. Yet, I chose to do so. That I would entertain the idea of marrying a man who isn't following the Lord and leading me closer to Him, much less one who doesn't even believe He is real, confirms that my walk with the Lord was still new and under-developed. I moved forward and married him anyway. I was grateful for the opportunity to be reconciled, but I had no idea what would lie ahead.

The struggle is real when you are dating a non-believer, and there is even more heartache when you are yoked to one. At first, things didn't seem to be bad, and there were not a whole lot of issues. As time went on and I began to seek the Lord in a deeper and more consistent manner, things began to show signs of strain. The closer I drew to the Lord, the farther apart I grew from all worldly things, including my husband. I no longer wanted to do the things I used to do: drink, hang out in bars, curse, and all the ways of the flesh. These things became distasteful to me, unpleasant, and surely unfulfilling. Yet, he was fine with it all; he drank just about every day, and this became a real issue for me. During our three years, apart, I had bought my own home and was back on my feet. My two children and I were doing well, and God was moving mightily in my heart and life. But, I still believed it was best to be with him again.

After dating for a little while, he moved in with us, and about a year later we were engaged. Three months into our engagement, I got pregnant. This was not planned, and I remember having very mixed feelings about the pregnancy. I already saw some very glaring signs that this relationship was not quite what I had hoped it would be. The real, raw motives of why I wanted to be back together were becoming very apparent. My walk with Christ was becoming deeper, and my relationship with Him was growing by leaps and bounds. He was doing good work in me, and I was getting to know Him. I loved being a mother, but I was so afraid I wouldn't have any more love to give to another child. My greatest desire was for my children to know deep down how much I loved and adored them. I began to ask God how in the world I was going to love this baby, and whether I would have more love to give than I already gave to Tayler and Derek. *Where will I find the energy to do this all over again?*

I was torn between the elation of being a mom again and the doubts that troubled me at the thought of starting all over again. I was also very concerned about him. He never wanted children, and here we were planning a wedding and the arrival of a baby. All the red flags were waving, wildly waving. I have never endured a more abusive relationship. He was a stark, vivid reminder of the disrespectful treatment I received from my father. He exhibited many of the selfish, narcissistic traits of my father. I never forced my beliefs on him. Never did I attempt to force-feed Christ into his heart. In fact, I stifled my belief and love of the Lord for his sake. I merely tried to walk in who I was becoming. Going to church on Sundays was now a constant for me. I remained respectful of his non-belief, even at the expense of hiding mine. His treatment of me was far less respectful. He was threatened by my love for God. He became verbally abusive, getting in my face and telling me, "There is no F'ing God." He would say that everyone who believed in God was a stupid idiot. I was slowly but surely being degraded by a man I called my husband, a man who claimed to love me. I knew my life and my soul were in deep trouble.

Planning our wedding was a complete catastrophe. I was not permitted to have a pastor perform our ceremony. We had an "officiator", and every single word he was to speak that day was scrutinized by him to be sure that God was not mentioned. Thinking back, I am horrified and so upset that as a Christian and lover of God, I allowed this and moved forward with marrying this man. But, I did. I was praying and believing God would touch him and soften his heart to break him down. I was praying he would become respectful of my beliefs and extend love and kindness towards me. Even if we didn't agree about the Lord, I prayed that we could somehow still love each other and co-exist in peace. I remember the day we had an appointment to go to the wedding venue. His parents were picking us up, and as he came upstairs, it was clear he had been drinking. I was so embarrassed. He was rude, disrespectful, and clearly did not want to be there. I can only imagine what his parents must have been thinking that day. I married him in May 2007. On September 29, 2007, I gave birth to our daughter, Ava Grace. Her birth gave me a reprieve, a distraction if you will, from his abuse as he became focused on Ava. But, it didn't last long.

The emotional abuse, drinking, and pot smoking became a real issue in our relationship. I was getting closer to God, and his choices and abuse were damaging my spirit every day. His presence was making me ill. I felt like I was living with the enemy himself, and, indeed, I was. The Word asks us in 2 Corinthians 6:14, "What fellowship does light have with darkness?" It has none. There was no peace in our home and no real love outside of the love we had for our daughter. Our physical relationship suffered, which was all he cared about. He treated me badly, emotionally abused me in so many ways, and then wondered why I wouldn't be intimate with him. God was vividly revealing my husband's shallowness to me. Women do not (and should not) feel compelled to be intimate with a person who is continually beating them up emotionally. I could not give of myself to a person who was not nurturing my heart and spirit.

God was showing me why it was not His will for this man to be my husband. God was nowhere in this marriage from the beginning. God did not choose this man; I did. This union was never ordained by God. I was living in Hell on Earth, but I still wanted things to work out. I tried to function the best I could, but my spirit was becoming damaged and beaten down. I spent countless evenings upstairs in my oldest daughter's room when she was with her dad. I would go there and cry out to God. I would lay there and ask God to please get me through another day of abuse. I would put earphones in and listen to worship music, allowing the Holy Spirit to comfort me, protect me, and help me to get some rest. He would often open the bedroom door and scream disrespectful things up the stairs about me and my love for God. At first, I would fight back, cry, and plead for him to stop. After months and months, I simply ran out of energy and surrendered it all to God. I in no way wanted a divorce, as I did not want another broken family. But, I was dying on the inside. This person was not my husband; this was not the man I desired, nor the man that God told me I was worth having. He was not the man God told me would adore me, cherish me, nurture me, and be my rock, my soft place to land. God was showing me that He needed me to rely on Him and His love. He needed me to put Him first. He was also reminding me that the man He chose for me would never treat me this way; the man He prepared and created for me wouldn't be capable of this deplorable treatment. He told me that the man He had for me was mature, kind, loving, respectful, Godly, sweet, selfless, nurturing, and so much more. At that moment, I simply wept in realizing that God's love for me was so deep and so real that He was keeping me this whole time. He knew I would be facing these challenges and heartaches. He tried to guide me away from it all, but I hadn't been obedient. God was still watching over me, still in control, still doing good work in me, and He knew I didn't have the strength to leave. He knew I would have remained there getting beaten up daily. But, God said, "NO, NO, NO… enough is enough!"

One day I came home from work, and he was gone. I walked around the house, weeping in disbelief. Not only did he take his clothes, but he took the television off the wall and my bed. If you ask him, it was his; after all, he had bought it. That pretty much tells the story of how disconnected we were and how far away we were from ever being real partners. The man who called himself my husband chose to give this example to not only our daughter but to my two children. It was an eye-opening blow to my heart that this was how he treated the mother of his child. I began to see and understand that this was way deeper than him not being a believer. Even people who don't believe in God know how to be kind, loving, and respectful. To me, my husband was evil. I sat in the space where my bed had stood, and I wept for hours… crying out to God, "Now what, God? Now what?"

Roadblock II: Second Divorce

"Do not be yoked together with unbelievers. For what do
righteousness and wickedness have in common?
Or what fellowship can light have with
darkness?" (2 Corinthians 6:14)

"And we know that all things work together for good
to them that love God, to them who are the called
according to his purpose." (Romans 8:28)

He moved out and set himself up in an apartment nearly 30
minutes away from Ava and me. His plan was to "work" on the
marriage while being separated. I ignorantly agreed to that. I was
willing to do anything to not have another broken family at all costs.
Nothing changed with him being gone; he left us high and dry with
a mortgage to pay all by myself. So I lost another home that I had
worked hard to buy for my children and me. Again, I packed up
my life, my kids packed up their lives, and I felt lost in the fog of
displacement that had become an all-too-familiar feeling. I rented
a house close to my kids' school, and I tried to pick up the pieces
of my shattered world again.

You can't successfully work on a relationship/marriage when you
are not living in the same home. We were living separate lives, and I
asked God what I should do. I know this relationship was not what
God desired for me. I did not believe that time apart would change
anything. I knew, deep down, that it was the beginning of the end.
He, on the other hand, thought it was just fine. He was emotionally
unavailable to me and always had been so this arrangement was
comfortable for him. He didn't have "to be" anything to me on

a daily basis. We occasionally talked on the phone and saw each other during the drop off times he had our daughter. He had no plans to get a divorce, and he would have remained in this state of living forever. But it was not okay for me. This was not a marriage. This was barely a friendship. We shared nothing together and were becoming more disconnected with each passing day.

One weekend evening when he had our daughter, I made my usual call to say hello to her and check in. There was no answer when I called, so I waited and called again; again no answer. I attempted a few more times after that; still nothing. Finally, after countless attempts, he answered the phone. I could tell he was drunk. I immediately asked where Ava was. He was very disrespectful and began to cuss me out, telling me not to worry about it. I was absolutely outraged to find out he was at a wedding, drunk, and would not tell me where my daughter was. Finally, he told me that she was with his parents. I abruptly hung up on him and called his parents to tell them under no circumstances were they to take my daughter back to him when he was home from the wedding. They always defended him, even when it was 100 percent wrong to do so. They told me they would talk with him and see what was going on. That was NOT going to work for this Mama. I got right in my car and drove to his apartment, knowing they would be meeting him there soon with my daughter. I arrived there to find his parents and my little girl standing outside his apartment door, knocking and knocking, waiting for him to answer. I approached them and told them they could knock all night long, but I was taking my daughter home. They were not cooperating at all and did not see the wrong in the choice they were making not to allow me to take her in light of the situation. I didn't want to upset my daughter, so I tried to keep calm and to not escalate the situation. I calmly said, "We are going home now," and just as I moved towards her, he opened the door.

He was visibly drunk and had obviously passed out, which is why he hadn't been answering. We all entered the apartment, and my only goal was to get my daughter and go. He told me that I was not permitted to take her since it was "his day" with her. I told him that I was taking her for the night, and when he slept it off and was sober in the morning, I would bring her back. His parents were not helping at all. He began to yell at me and get in my face. I was becoming afraid, but I was not leaving there without my daughter. He began yelling in my face, and then he picked me up and threw me out the door. I nearly fell down the flight of stairs outside his apartment. At that moment, all that mattered to me was getting my daughter out of there. I immediately called the police. His parent sat back and watched the whole thing. They kept telling him to sit down and calm down while they sat there and watched him throw me out the door, in front of their grand-daughter. Neither of them stood up to physically help me or stop him. I was appalled at their lack of integrity and inability to do the right thing in spite of this being their son. The police came and kept me separated from him. My daughter was still inside the apartment with him, his parents, and one police officer. I was outside with the other officer. I gave him the account of what had happened, and the next thing I knew he was being escorted out of the apartment, handcuffed. I had never been involved in any domestic violence before, so I had no idea that it was a routine procedure that anyone accused of domestic violence goes to jail. All I had wanted was help from the cops to get my daughter out of there. He went to jail, and my precious little girl and I went to our new home to sleep. We didn't have our beds there yet. But my heart didn't want to go to our old house where the reminder of all that was wrong was so heavy and apparent. I made us a bed on the floor with blankets. All I wanted to do was comfort her, hold her, and assure her that all was okay and she was safe. I lay there and wept, thanking God that He got us home safely; and, indeed, He was there with us. His presence was in the room, and I placed my fears, my heartache, my everything in His hands at that moment. I rested in His loving arms. My daughter and I were sheltered under His wings that night. It was a tangible knowing; He saw us clearly, deeply and He cared.

I am Enough and So Are You

"Look at the birds of the air; they neither sow, nor reap,
nor gather and yet your Heavenly Father feeds them.
Aren't you far more value than they are?" (Matthew 6:26)

"Whenever you feel unloved, unimportant, or insecure,
remember to whom you belong." (Ephesians 2:19-22)

For as far back as I can remember, I've longed for my dad to notice
me. I have memories of trying anything just to get him to see me
and to spend time with me. I wanted to walk into a room and see
his eyes light up, for him to sweep me up on his lap and tell me just
how much he adored me. I wanted him to tell me how special I
was to him, how unique I was, how amazing I was to him. I wanted
him to tell me that I was enough just being Laura. I wanted him
to be proud of me. I wanted him to tell me and show me what
love looked like. I desperately wanted to feel love from him and to
know that I was precious to him. These things simply never came.
These moments never happened for me. I applied myself, worked
hard, excelled in school and tried to be the best daughter I could
be. I thought that if I came as close to perfection as could, maybe,
just maybe, I would gain his attention and earn his affection. But
my efforts changed nothing in him and only served to deflate me
further, causing an endless search for self-worth. I thought that if
my own father wasn't moved by me and didn't see me as worthy
of love, affection, and attention, then who in the world would?
Something must be drastically wrong with me.

So much damage had occurred during my childhood, and I had
buried it deep down in my soul. It was too painful to face the truth

that the man I called Daddy and adored simply didn't adore me or delight in my presence. No matter what I did, how hard I tried, or how much I wanted him to, he never noticed me. I didn't know it then, but I now know this lack has stolen years from me and cost me more than I ever imagined it could. Sometimes we don't realize the devastation our hearts have endured until we come face-to-face with the real issue, to the root of a thing. My dad is the source of much of my heartache, and my search for his love, affection, and attention has affected every intimate relationship I've ever been in. To this day, the little girl in me has moments of yearning to feel those things from him. I've spent the better part of my adulthood grieving this loss, allowing it to trip me up in more ways than I care to even admit at times. It has paralyzed me in my creativity and in my motivation to become all that God has called me to be in this world. It has created in me the fear that I am not enough for anything or anyone, and I am plagued by thoughts that I am not enough as a mom, a friend, a wife, or a woman. If my own father didn't see my worth and didn't notice me, if I am not enough for him, then who then could I possibly be enough for?

It has been an uphill climb and a battle in my soul that has left me exhausted, wounded, and at times completely lost. But, God found me and began to massage my heart back to life. He, of course, knew my pain; He was there all along, so He handles me with care. He knew I needed His love, but He also knew I would have trouble trusting Him and His love. So, He graciously met me just where I was the day I was saved, and every day since then He has met me with a tenderness I can't put into words. He soothes me; He calms me, and yet He pushes me to the naked edge of my fears. He tells me every single day how much He loves me, and I cry every time in the knowledge and truth that I am truly loved, adored, and noticed. God sees me! In times of heartache, I find my strength in God. In His presence, I am free to be me and free to stand boldly against the troubles of life and this world. In His love, I find the acceptance I've never known before.

In His wisdom, my soul can finally know and feel the truth of who I am. Only He can sustain me, and only He can give me the strength to get up when all I want to do is stay down. Only He can reveal the beauty of my being, the worth of my soul, and the ugliness that intertwines them both. In the stillness, when I allow myself to listen to Him, to life, I am reminded of the blessing that merely exists in waking to another day. I have endured many heartbreaking moments and seasons in my life, yet I press on knowing that all the seeds I have planted will reap a harvest in due time. I've learned more about myself and my worth, and I have shaken off the belief that I somehow don't deserve more or deserve better; I now know I deserve the best. I belong to a God who assures me every day of what I should and should not accept from others or from myself.

As a Christian, I am called to forgive, to love, and to turn the other cheek. I will continue to strive toward that goal each day. But, I am not called to remain in a place that violates my heart, instead of protecting it. I give my wounds to God as He is the only one who can truly heal me. And I walk with my head held high as a redeemed woman of God: Sweet but strong, tender but tough, refined but sharp, direct but feminine. I am a warrior. Yes, a warrior is who I am, and that is who you are! He loves me 100 percent, heart and soul, and each day I hear him whisper, "Laura, my beautiful daughter, you are enough!"

GROUND ZERO

"Forget the former things; do not dwell on the past.

See, I am doing a new thing! Now it springs up;
do you not perceive it?

I am making a way in the wilderness and streams
in the wasteland." (Isaiah 43:18-20)

The definition of life is the sequence of physical and mental experiences that make up the existence of an individual according to the Merriam-Webster dictionary. This is what I am left with...a series of physical and mental experiences that have made up my life to this point. I sit down and begin to wonder how I arrived here: Two failed marriages, walking with the Lord, yet still carrying and feeling emotions that I have had since I was a little girl. What was happening here? I felt a sense of that familiar panic, but it was coupled with a greater sense of peace this time. I began to think about "arriving", that elusive point in our lives that we seem to be trying to "get to". Our arrival is different for each of us. For some it's a career goal, getting married, having children, or buying a house or car; for others, it's all of these. But what does arriving really mean, and why in the world are we so consumed with it? I was beginning a deep soul search, and it was time; whether I was ready or not, it was coming. The following poem is about God and how He saw me, how He loves me, how He continues to reveal the plans and thoughts He has towards me.

He said I was an Angel;

He said, "What a beauty to behold!"

He said, "What a beautiful heart you have;

I hope to have, to hold."

What He saw, He made known.

What He felt, He was sure to show.

What He touched, He never left alone.

What He loved, He kept aglow.

He said I was an Angel;

He asked if He could take me home

To keep me forever,

To surround me with love,

And that He would never roam.

He said I was an Angel;

This I began to believe.

I may not have felt it was Him,

But He surely felt it was ME.

BROKEN BEAUTY

"It is not fancy hair, gold jewelry, or fine clothes that should
make you beautiful. No, your beauty should come from
inside you—the beauty of a gentle and quiet spirit.
That beauty will never disappear and it is worth
very much to God." (I Peter 3:3-4)

"Perhaps this is the moment for which you
were created." (Esther 4:14)

God always has a plan. There is always beauty that emerges from
our pain. When I look back to all the darkest, most challenging
times in my life, I can now recognize that God's hand of grace
was with me through it all. I believe that God can work best in
adverse times, but we also must allow our faith and trust in Him
to rise-up to a new level. Even when what we see looks so grim,
and the way seem impossible, we must hold tight to His word and
His promises. During one of my darkest days in which I was filled
with so much sadness about all the losses I had suffered as a child
and as an adult, all the brokenness that had occurred in my life,
God showed up in a mighty way and changed my life. He came and
revealed to me my purpose; my personal purpose was birthed out
of my own journey of pain and searching for worth. I woke up on
a Sunday morning in 2014 with a heavy heart. I was overwhelmed
with the sadness about all the disappointments and losses in my
life. All I wanted to do was stay in bed and cry. I made my mind
up that I wasn't going to church, and I, indeed, was just going to
cry all day. That sounded like a plan to me. But God had other
plans for me that day. As I was lying there crying, my spirit would
not settle. I kept feeling the tug to pick up a pen and paper. I

fought this tug for several hours until I reluctantly decided to get up for that pen and paper. I sat there not knowing what I needed to write, but the Lord knew, and I began to write. Today is not a bad day, maybe it is not a good day either, but it is a Day of Grace. These words woke me up to the realization that every day we have God's grace. From there, God began to pour into me. A women's event called Day of Grace was birthed out of this very dark day in my life. God gave me all the details: the name, the place, the time, the theme, the people who were to be a part of the day, ALL OF THE DETAILS. And, on September 13th, 2014, Day of Grace happened. It was a day for women to come and bask in the love of our Heavenly Father, fellowship with other women, and it was a chance to be refreshed in His amazing love. The Holy Spirit was so present on that day. We cried, laughed, sang, and shared. As the event was ending, a lady asked if she could come up and share something with us. I, of course, said yes. She began to weep and told us that she was planning to commit suicide the night before this event. She received an invitation to Day of Grace from one of her friends, and for some reason, she decided to come. At that moment, I knew I was doing exactly what God desired for me to do. If she was the only woman who came to Day of Grace, it was all worth it. A life had been saved, a spirit was inspired, and hope was restored to this beautiful woman. I often wonder what would have happened if I would not have said YES to God when He asked me to have this event. I am so grateful to God for choosing me; I believe He knew I would say YES. This was the beginning of what has now become a yearly event, and we are embarking on our fifth annual Day of Grace this year, 2018! What is even more amazing is that an entire women's ministry, Broken Beauty Ministries, was birthed after the first Day of Grace. God had even bigger plans for me, and in one of my darkest times, He showed up. He poured into me and revealed to me my purpose.

Often we become comfortable in our brokenness; we struggle and even fight off becoming healed. It is like we become friends with the pain, and it begins to feel normal to the point that healing feels foreign to us. God provides healing and wholeness. It is my heart's desire to instill the truth of who we are and what we deserve and to shine light on the darkness that so many of us are walking in. We must shed the lie that we are not enough, that we are not worthy of greatness, and that we can't overcome pain and heartache. These are all lies! The truth is that you are a beautiful butterfly, a tender root destined for greatness. I believe as young girls we crave love and attention from our earthly fathers. It is essential to our well-being and our hearts. When this is missing, lacking, we set out on a never-ending journey to find this lost father love, but we end up searching in places that lead only to more heartache and pain. In the end, we give up our innocence, our hearts, and parts of our souls to consistently empty, unfulfilling experiences. Some search to fill this void with drugs, alcohol, sex, etc. One day I woke up and counted all the losses I had suffered in my search, the parts of my heart that were gone, the parts of my soul that I freely gave away with nothing to gain in return. I had essentially suffered a loss with each and every sexual encounter. I began to ask myself why in the world I kept participating in something that I had absolutely nothing to gain from: no joy, no peace, no sense of fulfillment, no edification, nothing. I walked away each time with less of my heart and soul, and I could no longer afford to do that. I was simply too important and too special to allow this to go on. My Father in Heaven spoke these simple words to me: "I created you for more; you are precious in my sight." And He feels the same way about each of you. You are worth so much to God that He sent His one and only son to die on the cross for you! Yes, YOU; even if you were the only one on this planet, He would have done the same unmatched act of LOVE.

DEAR LAURA

"God is within her, she will not fall." (Psalm 46:5)

"She is clothed with strength and dignity, and she laughs
without fear of the future." (Proverbs 31:25)

I often wonder what I would tell "little girl Laura" if I had a chance
to sit down and talk with her. Knowing all that I know now, and
having gone through all the heartaches, challenges, good times,
bad times, and everything in between, I wonder what I would say
to that little girl. It would not be my intent to necessarily change
the course of her life, nor to reveal to her all that she would endure,
but, I do know I would first and foremost tell her how much she is
loved and adored, and that even when the people in her life were
not capable of giving her this love, love was still surrounding her.
I would be available to her, not to speak but just to listen to the
innermost yearnings of her heart. I would tell her that life will
bring challenges, heartache, joy, pain, laughter, and tears. I would
tell her that life will bring you to times of isolation, despair, and
hardship (financially, spiritually, physically, and emotionally.) There
will be dark times when she will feel as though she is lost and
abandoned in a cruel and desolate world. There will be times when
she questions every truth she has ever been told and times when
she will wonder why she was born and what she was brought into
this world to do. There will be times that she will feel like giving up
on everything and everyone; and she will wonder if she will ever
feel "full" and feel the love, compassion, and connection she longs
for. There will be times that she will suffer from anxiety, panic,
and depression and not even want to or be able to leave the house.
There will be times that she will be so filled with guilt from her

past mistakes that she will find little worth in herself, which will only cause her to search for acceptance in all the wrong ways with all the wrong people. I have just painted a fairly grim picture for her, so at this point, I'm pretty sure she will be feeling horrible about life and what's to come.

But, I will also tell her how beautiful life is; how she will experience so much joy in becoming a mother. I will tell her of all the little glimpses of God's grace and love that she will receive and feel even in her darkest times. I will tell her of all the sunrises she will be blessed to see, and that joy does come in the morning. I will tell her that there will be days when just feeling the sun kiss her face will give her all she needs to endure the day and her heartaches. I will tell her about the laughter she will encounter; the fun times she will have watching her children grow up; the immense pleasure she will get in seeing their smiles and their happiness. I will tell her about the overwhelming peace she will feel when her toes are in the sand, and she looks out at the ocean, and at that moment the goodness of God, His majesty and the depth of His love will overtake her spirit. I will tell her about never giving up. I will tell her about the absolute wonder of life, the way she will feel when God speaks tenderly to her heart and says, "I AM HERE ALWAYS; I LOVE YOU." I will tell her how her children's faces, their hugs, and their kisses will leave her speechless, even breathless sometimes, as they remind her of God's grace and mercy. In these moments, life will make sense to her. I will tell her that one fine day, the man God chose for her will arrive, and he will be more than she ever imagined. I will tell her that beauty is in her brokenness; it always has been. I will tell her that when moving, when breathing seems difficult, to keep walking and taking steps, for each step will lead her closer to God. She is destined to make it back home.

HE TAKES ME BACK

"God demonstrates His own love for us in this, while we were still sinners, Christ died for us." (Romans 5:8)

"The Lord is my strength and my shield." (Psalm 28:7)

"Be strong and courageous. Do not be afraid; do not be discouraged, for the Lord your God is with you wherever you go." (Joshua 1:9)

Such an awesome God He is! When I think about where He has brought me from and what He has brought me through, I can't help but cry. I am so humbled by His love, His undeniable love for every part of me. Still, I have times that I question His love, as truly accepting love has been a challenge for me. It didn't matter how love was given to me or shown to me; I simply couldn't fully receive or trust that it was real. On the rare times I would open up and let my guard down to trust, man would let me down, crush my heart, take away love, and leave me with the pain of loss, wondering how I was going to recover yet again. I did what I always did: I gave myself again, hoping this time that this one would be my savior, this one would fill me up. Getting naked physically never gave me a thing, nor did it ever heal any part of my heart—and it never will. I first needed to become spiritually naked with God and then with myself. Only then could I bear my soul and inch my way to healing and becoming vulnerable with myself and others. Vulnerability can be scary if we let it be, yet this is the very place where we need to be to allow our souls to be fully known and to allow our hearts to fully open, fearlessly sharing our innermost feelings with God first and then with another human being. True freedom arises, and a love like you've never known before will organically blossom....

Often we run from God, from the truth, and from life and its challenges & heartaches. Somehow we think that we can simply act like nothing is going on and nothing needs to be faced; maybe if we just don't talk about it, it will disappear; that somehow the pain will just vanish. The truth is we just bury it, and everything buried eventually gets unearthed. Even as believers, we have moments, seasons, and sometimes we simply run out of hope and faith, and we begin to question God and His faithfulness. We are still human, but thankfully God always is waiting with open arms to take us back into His loving care, His loving arms.

FORGIVENESS

"If we confess our sins, he is faithful and just and will
forgive us our sins and purify us from all
unrighteousness." (1 John 1:9)

"For if you forgive other people when they sin against you,
your heavenly Father will also forgive you. But if you do
not forgive others their sins, your Father will not
forgive your sins." (Matthew 6:14-15)

At this point, I was in desperate need of forgiving myself and
everyone who had let me down, hurt me, or broken my heart. That
needed to begin with my father. I entered grief counseling with
the most amazing counselor ever. She made me look at things that
my heart just couldn't and didn't want to feel: pain that had been
buried for years. This pain was sabotaging my chances at healing
and of being able to experience real love. My counselor asked me
to do a timeline of my life, which consisted of writing down every
memory that I had, every single tiny morsel of a memory. It was
the most painful experience for me. I sat with a pen and paper
and began to review my entire life from the earliest memory to
the latest one. I wept from the depths of my soul, and at that
moment, healing began. I wanted so desperately to allow myself to
feel again, to love again, and to be loved—and it was time.

God spoke clearly that enough was enough. Forgiveness is a
difficult thing for many people. I believe that we tend to think that
we are somehow condoning the treatment if we make the decision
to forgive those that have caused us pain. Pain is personal. Nobody
can understand the real, raw pain of another human being. We can

empathize but never to the level that it was experienced by the recipient of the hurt. I believe there is a role that the person who caused the pain plays in the forgiveness journey, and the person that caused the hurt often does understand the gravity of the pain. We have all heard the phrase, "Hurt people hurt people." My healing did not fully begin until I understood this truth. I was holding people hostage for hurting me, but the reality was that they, too, were dealing with their own demons and pains.

We are all a product of our upbringing, and none of us came from a perfect family, free from drama, pain, and challenges. We must remember that our parents, too, have come from where they have come from and function as such. Where we are born into is not where we are destined to remain. We are to rise above and gain ground on the dysfunction we came from, and it begins with being born again. As we see in Jesus, our perfect example of forgiveness, we too are called to forgive those who trespass against us and hurt us. It requires us to take a deep look within to see our imperfections and times that we have caused others pain. The most beautiful story of redemption lies in knowing that we are forgiven, for without fully accepting that we are forgiven, redemption seems like some aloof, unattainable dream. In his struggle, Jesus surrendered. God didn't let the cup pass, but He gave Jesus strength to drink the cup. We each have a cup that we don't want to drink. The struggle to find a job, challenges with our children, our health, heartbreak, brokenness, are all cups we are asked to drink from. Forgiving others is a deep cup that we struggle to sip from. But God is waiting for us to surrender it all to Him. God gave Jesus the strength to endure the cross, so certainly He can and will give us the strength to endure whatever we are facing and to drink the cup that is before us today. I choose to surrender and take the limits off the amazing God I serve and say, "Nevertheless, Your will, not mine."

While finishing up this book, my father, who had suffered addiction for many years, fell seriously ill and was hospitalized in the ICU.

This was not the first time that he had been sick enough to be sent to the hospital, but this time I knew the Lord was saying something must change. He did not know where he was or who I was. It was a very difficult thing to accept that he was so ill he didn't know me. I came home one night after visiting him and wrote this:

All my life I have longed for you to be strong, to be a man I could lean on, a man who would guide me into being the best woman I could be. I longed for you to embrace me with the deep love of a father for his daughter. I longed for you to smile at my achievements, to cheer me on, to lift me up when I fell, to wipe away my tears, to tell me that everything, every little thing, was going to be okay. I've wanted your love for so long, Dad, and now as I look at your frail body lying in this hospital bed, as I see you lose the hope to live, to not even know who I am because of your unfortunate addiction, I'm faced with the stark and heartbreaking truth that you've been searching for love and acceptance your whole life. You are a man housing a broken little boy's heart. A little boy that is so full of pain; a little boy crying out for something only God can provide. I now understand that you couldn't give me what you didn't have inside. I find myself wanting to nurture you, to be strong for you, to embrace you with the love of a daughter for her father. I want to tell you that every little thing is going to be okay. I find myself filled with such compassion and forgiveness that I know without a doubt God is in our midst; God is restoring and healing.

La Dolce Vita (Life is Sweet)

"Blessed is she who believed that the Lord would fulfill
His promises to her." (Luke 1:45)

"Mightier than waves of the sea is His love
for you." (Psalm 93:4)

La dolce vita in Italian means "life is sweet". I honestly believe that despite all the heartaches, challenges, and disappointments, life is still so very sweet. I feel it in the touch of my lover, in the voice of my children, in the beauty of a flower, in the smell of a newborn baby, in the taste of a delicious plate of food, in the quiet of the evening, in the joy of the morning, in the sip of a good cup of coffee, in the eyes of my elderly neighbor, in the shine of the sun, in the sparkle of the stars, and so much more.... I find life's sweetness the most in love. It all comes down to love. After all, we were created by God, and God is love. We are love; love in its purest form is in us; our innate desire is to love and be loved. When I sit back in the stillness to examine my past, my losses, my relationships, my joys, and my triumphs, love has been the central theme of it all. Why wouldn't it be? The one, beautiful, unmatched sacrifice the Lord gave us was all for love. You simply can't know God or be in a relationship with Him and not know love and desire to freely give it out. As my pastor says, "We are to be love dispensers." When you have truly experienced the depth of God's love, His mercy, and His grace, you won't be able to walk around in negativity or have a crotchety, complaining spirit. His love will compel you to love, to give, to see the sweetness of this beautiful thing we call life. You will find yourself in awe of just breathing, being able to wake up to a new day, and to the privilege of being alive. No, things will not always be easy, for life will be life; it will bring sadness, loss, and challenges for sure. But God promises to always be near us and walk with us through it all. When you know and accept the love of our Heavenly Father and really allow what He gave up for you to penetrate your heart, you will never be the same. You will love differently; you will extend forgiveness more easily; you will show grace more often; you will delight in and notice the small things; you will be grateful; you will be touched to the core of your heart by the sacrifice He made for you to be alive; and you, too, will know and truly experience that Life is so very sweet.

I read this profound statement about love made by C.S. Lewis:

"To love at all is to be vulnerable. Love anything, and your heart will certainly be wrung and possibly broken. If you want to make sure of keeping it intact, you must give your heart to no one, not even an animal. Wrap it carefully around hobbies, your job, and little luxuries; avoid all entanglements; lock it up safe in the casket or the coffin of selfishness. But, in that casket, safe, dark, motionless, airless, it will change. It will not be broken; it will become unbreakable, impenetrable, irredeemable. The alternative to tragedy, or at least to the risk of tragedy, is damnation. The only place outside of Heaven where you can be perfectly safe from all the dangers and heartaches of love is Hell."

And this one from L.R. Knost:

"Do not be dismayed by the brokenness of the world. All things break. And all things can be mended. Not with time, as they say, it is with intention. So, Go Love intentionally, extravagantly, unconditionally. The broken world waits in darkness for the light that is YOU!"

I choose LOVE every single time, in every situation…ALWAYS!

BREATHE AGAIN

"You are altogether beautiful, my darling, beautiful
in every way." (Song of Solomon 4:7)

"The Lord will fight for you, you need
only be still." (Exodus 14:14)

I have loved and been fascinated by butterflies, particularly monarch
butterflies, since I was a little girl. I was blessed by a story I read
about butterfly wings, and I want to share it with you:

> One day a man came upon the cocoon of a butterfly.
> He saw the butterfly struggling to force its body through
> a small opening in the cocoon. After several hours, it
> seemed the butterfly stopped making progress. It
> appeared as if it had gotten as far as it could, and it
> could not go any further. To be helpful, the man took
> a pair of scissors and snipped off the remaining bit of
> the cocoon. The butterfly then emerged easily, but it
> had a swollen body and small, shriveled wings. The man
> continued to watch the butterfly because he expected
> that at any moment, the wings would enlarge and expand
> to be able to support the body, which would contract
> in time. Neither happened. In fact, the butterfly spent
> the rest of its life crawling around with a swollen body
> and shriveled wings. It was never able to fly. The man,
> in his kindness and haste, did not understand that the
> butterfly had to struggle through the tiny opening of the
> restrictive cocoon, as it is nature's way of forcing fluid
> from the body of the butterfly into its wings. This way,
> it would be ready for flight once freed from the cocoon.

As I read this, it reminded me of the struggles we face and how they are often needed for our growth and development. Overcoming life's obstacles makes us stronger and wiser than we would be without them. Imagine for one minute where you would be right now if you had never faced obstacles. You wouldn't have the same beliefs, morals, or values that you have. You would not be as mentally strong. You would not have had your chance to spread your wings and fly! I wouldn't be me if I hadn't lived through all that I have endured. It's made me stronger. It's made me responsible. It's made me go after a better life for myself. It's made me love better. It's helped me accept people exactly where they are. And most of all, it's enabled me to encourage others. Next time you are faced with a challenge or obstacle, don't take the scissors and try to cut your way out of that situation. Learn what you need to learn. Grow. Know that you are not the first person to endure it, and you won't be the last. With each passing struggle, you will fly higher and higher.

Sometimes in life, we are blessed and sent someone who helps us to see that we have wings and that we were indeed created to fly. I have been blessed to have been sent someone who has done this very thing for me. Sometimes it is hard to convey what we feel in our hearts for someone, especially when we are still in the process of healing. But, I choose love, and with that, I must express my heart. I pray that the depths of my love and appreciation will be both captured and received from the bottom of my heart. What you mean to me is more than I'm able to express in words, but I will give it my all and try to do just that. I've always been a fighter only because I was forced to be. Now I have been shown by you that I no longer need to fight. I can really step out of survival mode. I'm not sure how you are different; it seems most of the men in my life have recognized this about me. But you have penetrated my heart in a way that no other man ever has. I'm amazed by your ability to see right through to my innermost pains and disappointments, as well as to recognize all of my modes of protecting myself.

59

I have lashed out in anger so many times, and each time you came to me with understanding and an overwhelming desire to help me understand myself and to overcome these patterns of dysfunction that have plagued my soul for quite some time. Most of the time, I continued to fight even you, the one who was desperately trying to help me heal. You know me better than I know myself in many ways. Before I met you, I prayed that the Lord would send me a man who loved Jesus. That was my one and only criteria. So, of course, I was more than excited to meet you and find out that you believe in the Lord. What I wasn't aware of are all the other amazing things you had to share with me. You have had more patience with me and my brokenness than anyone I've ever allowed to get to know me even a little. You continue to press in, to give me the green light to give you this part of my heart that I have kept hidden and safe from everyone, at times even myself. I have pushed away that green light many times; pushed away your patient heart that tells me I am safe only because being safe has never been real for me.

Many times, I had believed my heart was in a safe place, and I could finally surrender the one part of my heart that I had closed off to everyone. It became a clear disappointment, and I was left even more broken than before. I no longer believed there would ever be a man who I could really trust with my whole heart (except Jesus); He alone has been the source of my strength and stability. Then came you…and my heart began to understand that my protection was only harming my heart, not healing it, and I was robbing myself of experiencing a real, deep love; a love that transcends physical attraction; a love that sees clear into the depths of one's pain and begins to compassionately unpack the baggage of many years of hurt and disappointment. I have fought you; fought your efforts on more than one occasion; in many instances, my fight came so naturally to me that the fortress around my heart was all I knew. Slowly, steadily, lovingly, and sometimes with a stern, bold slap in the face, you brought a light to my heart that it had only dreamed of and that I never thought was possible.

In my quest to protect and guard my heart, all the while desiring a connection with a man that penetrates all barriers and walls, I finally found a truth in you that simply humbles me and allows me to breathe deeply again; I am able to breathe in the reality of real love and the reality of unconditional patience and acceptance. Just as our Heavenly Father accepts us, flaws and all, you have opened not only my eyes but more importantly my heart. My heart had been on lockdown for more years than I even know. You and your love have unlocked the part of my heart that I have been desperately holding back my whole life. No matter what may come, you have it, and you deserve it. I prayed for you, I asked God for you, and He answered. Your love of Christ was my only request, and we know that God is able to go above and beyond all that we can ask or think, exceedingly, abundantly more. God has surely made a way and moved mountains to get us to where we are right now. You are a true answer to my prayer.

Resurrection/Redeemed

"For your Maker is your husband—

the Lord Almighty is his name—

the Holy One of Israel is your Redeemer;

he is called the God of all the earth." (Isaiah 54:5)

Present day: Here I am, finishing this book. I sit here humbled by what the Lord has done for me and where he has brought me from. I recognize that my search and my desire has always been for a family. I want to have a Godly husband, a best friend, a leader, a lover, a provider, and someone that I can share life with. I want to share all aspects of our lives: my children, his children (if he has any), our visions, as well as get a hold of a vision together as husband and wife. I want a relationship built on the solid foundation of the Lord, a relationship that doesn't include lies, manipulation, immaturity, or any other destructive behaviors. Sex should be the climax of intimacy, not the beginning of it. I have given myself sexually to men without having these other things, and the only thing that happened was more pain and more emptiness. I no longer have time for the nonsense, the games, the projects, or the wait. It's go-time, and I know that the Lord has already hand-picked this man for me, and I know that all this was preparing me to become the best I could be.

I had a very moving experience that helped me get to this point that I want to share with you. One day, I was at a friend's house, and she had some company over. One lady had her daughter Lilly

with her, who was about 2-years-old. She came right up to me to
say hello. She was so full of life, and I began to think:

She hasn't been hurt...yet.
She hasn't had her heart broken...yet.
She hasn't been lied to...yet.
She hasn't been cheated on...yet.
She hasn't been laughed at...yet.
She hasn't been judged...yet.
She hasn't been beaten...yet.
She hasn't been ridiculed...yet.
She hasn't been raped...yet.
She hasn't been called ugly...yet.
She hasn't been told she is not enough...yet.

I looked at her big, beautiful, blue eyes, and at that moment I
saw the absolute, pure innocence of her heart that had not yet
been tainted by this world. She had a heart and light that only
radiated its true nature: trust and belief. I knew it was God who
wanted me to see this, to really experience the truth in that exact
moment. It was like time stood still as He softly whispered to me,
"This is how I want you to be; this is who you are." I was in awe,
and this poem came to me:

A Man I Know

Let me tell you about a Man I know.

He washed away my sins, as white as snow.

He made me new; made me whole.

He gave me life; He saved my soul.

His love can't be matched.

Every hole in your heart won't just be patched;

He will remove all the pain

And leave you with everything to gain.

Just when you think you have nothing to restore,

He opens up Heaven and lets His love pour.

Every single day over you He sings.

Every hour only promises He brings.

He loves to love you, not for what you do;

He loves to love you, just because you are you.

He corrects you not because He is mad at you;

He corrects you so you learn not to hate you.

He brings life to the dead; His presence is our living bread.

He delivers your mind, so only His way will you find!

AND SO IT GOES

"Sing, O barren one, break forth into singing and cry aloud,
you who have not been in labor! For the children of the
desolate one will be more than the children of her who is
married," says the Lord. "Enlarge the place of your tent,
and let the curtains of your habitations be stretched out;
do not hold back; lengthen your cords and strengthen your
stakes. For you will spread abroad to the right and to the left,
and your offspring will possess the nations and will people
the desolate cities. "Fear not, for you will not be ashamed;
be not confounded, for you will not be disgraced; for you
will forget the shame of your youth, and the reproach of
your widowhood you will remember no more. For your
Maker is your husband, the Lord of hosts is His name;
and the Holy One of Israel is your Redeemer; he is
called the God of the whole earth. (Isaiah 54:1-6)

"See, I have already begun! Do you not see it? I will make
a pathway through the wilderness. I will create rivers
in the dry wasteland." (Isaiah 43:19)

"Let all you do be done in love." (I Corinthians 16:14)

It is Well With My Soul (Horatio Spafford)

Grander earth has quaked before, moved by
the sound of His voice.

Seas that are shaken and stirred

Can be calmed and broken for my regard.

Through it all, through it all,

My eyes are on you;

Through it all, through it all,

It is well.

Far be for me not to believe,

Even when my eyes can't see,

And this mountain that's in front of me

Will be thrown into the midst of the sea.

So let go, my soul, and trust in Him.

The waves and the wind still know His name

Through it all, through it all,

My eyes on are on you;

And it is well.

It is well…with me.

And so, the journey continues. In the stillness and quiet of this morning, as I write the last page of this book that God has entrusted me to write, I am reminded of the blessing that merely waking up to another day really is. This past year has been one of the most heartbreaking, yet one of the most inspiring years, of my life. I press on knowing that all the seeds I have planted will, in due time, reap a harvest for His glory. I've learned more about myself, more about my worth, and I have shaken off the lie that I somehow don't deserve the best. I belong to God, who assures me every day of what I should and should not accept. As a Christian, I am called to forgive, to love, and to turn the other cheek; I will continue to do this all the days of my life. I have learned to give my wounds to God as He is the only one who can really heal me. I now walk with my head held high as a Redeemed Woman of God: sweet but strong; tender but tough; refined but sharp; direct but feminine. I am a warrior. My heart has been deeply touched and changed by a love that can only be given by our Heavenly Father, my ultimate love, and no amount of gratitude will ever be enough to thank Him for all He has done for me, for my heart, and my very soul.

I encourage you to share your story…. Somebody needs to hear it, even if that somebody is only YOU!

WRITE YOUR STORY….

WRITE YOUR OWN STORY

WRITE YOUR OWN STORY